38 Ways to Entertain Your Babysitter

by Dette Hunter

art by Stephen MacEachern

Annick Press Ltd.
Toronto * New York * Vancouver

The Amazing Daisy

 Contents

Buttons, Bangles, and Beads

Fancy Hands

Space Snacks

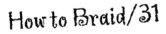

Did you hear the one...

To Charles, Amy, and Claire, my favorite space invaders.
—D.H.

To Ethan and Kylie, who always give their babysitters lots to do.
—S.M.

Some of the activities in this book require the use
of a microwave oven. Kids should always carry out
these activities under supervision.

Introduction

Babysitters and kids are a cool combo, but a day indoors with nothing special to do is a definite downer. Look out! Here comes fun with *38 Ways to Entertain Your Babysitter*.

First of all, it's a story, because a book is the best boredom beater there is. But, as our hero, Leo, knows, even a humongous pile of books isn't always enough. This book is more than a story. It has something to do on almost every page. That way, if you're reading along and suddenly decide that you can't resist the crunchy Millennium Munch bars that Leo whips up, presto!—you can make them yourself and come back to the story later.

The easy recipe and craft instructions for whatever you decide to do are right on the page. Pretty much everything you'll need to make them you can find around the house. These activities are really neat (if you get what I mean)—clean-up is simple, so the only surprises parents come home to will be good ones!

Leo, his little sister, Daisy, and their new babysitter make all kinds of magic. You can too. Turn an ordinary piece of bread into a butterfly sandwich, make a movie from a pile of paper or transform a tortilla into a hat (you can eat!). Before you know it, you'll have turned a boring old day into a totally fun time together.

Dette Hunter

"We've got big trouble, Hubble." I said.

Hubble thumped his tail. He was ready to hear all about it.

"We have a new babysitter for the whole day," I told him. "Before Mom left she said, 'Leo, I'm depending on you to make sure she has a good time and wants to come back.'

"I don't know anything about entertaining baby-sitters. I thought they had enough fun stuff in their back-packs to keep them busy for light-years.

"Mom is depending on us, Hubble. We have new frontiers to explore—babysitters and beyond!!"

The Hubble Space Telescope orbits 600 kilometers (375 miles) above the Earth, using state-of-the-art instruments to provide pictures of the universe.

My little sister, Daisy, and the babysitter had already started on a humongous pile of books. Somehow, I don't think reading about dancing ducks all day is what my mom meant by a good time. Daisy and I would have to come up with something a whole lot better.

"Here's our new babysitter. She has lots of silver rings and bracelets…even on her teeth! Her name's Helen after her grandmother but she thinks she's more of a Halley than a Helen and I do too," said Daisy, all in one breath.

Halley smiled and sure enough she had brand new shiny braces on her teeth.

I stuck out my hand and said, "My name's Leo, after my great-uncle, and I like to be called Leo, because that's my name. My mission is to make sure you have a good time."

"Cool," she said. "Let the games begin."

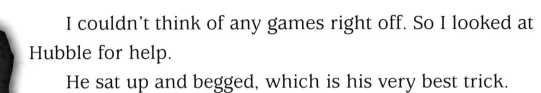 The Amazing Daisy

I couldn't think of any games right off. So I looked at Hubble for help.

He sat up and begged, which is his very best trick.

"I read you, Hubble," I said. "I'll do my famous space spinner trick!"

Magic Moon Spinner

YOU'LL NEED:
★ 3″ x 5″ (8 cm x 12 cm) piece of paper (an index card is perfect)
★ Marker
★ Straw
★ Clear tape

On one side of the paper draw an astronaut and on the other draw a large moon.

Fold the paper in half (width-wise), so your drawings are back to back.

Tape the straw to the back of one of the drawings.

Tape closed at the side.

Hold the straw between both hands and roll it back and forth quickly.

Watch the man land on the moon!

With a quick spin of my hands I made the man land on the moon!

Daisy always has to be the center of the universe. So I knew it wouldn't be long before she came up with a trick of her own.

Wizard Hat

YOU'LL NEED:
☆ 3 full sheets of newspaper
☆ Tape

Lay sheets of newspaper on a flat surface.

Treating the stack as if it were a single sheet of paper, roll and shape it into a large cone.

Tape the overlapping edge of the cone.

Simply fold the edge into the hat or roll up the bottom edge to make a band.

tape

fold in and tape

9

"I'm the Amazing Daisy, the Wizard of Scissors," she announced, "and before your very eyes, I will turn a plain piece of paper into a pretty pointy star! My magician's assistant, Halley, will help a little bit on the folds."

Daisy's Special Star

YOU'LL NEED:
★ A paper rectangle (a sheet of computer paper is fine)
★ Scissors

Always fold along the dotted line in the direction of the arrow.
1. Fold in half the short way. Crease.
2. Bring the lower right corner to the halfway point. Crease.
3. Fold the left edge over to the right. Crease.
4. Now fold the right edge over to the left. Crease.
5. Cut as shown.
6. Unfold.

Daisy unfolded an amazing star.

Tip:
Use stars to decorate wizard hat.

We all clapped. Daisy blooms when she has an audience.

"And now, lady and gentledog," I said, "Daisy and I will perform our famous falling star trick. We will attempt the impossible…."

"Oh no, Lee-o," Daisy interrupted, "I don't want to be a wizard anymore."

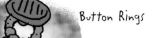

Buttons, Bangles, and Beads

"Now, I want to be a babysitter," Daisy said. "I want to have rings and bracelets and fancy fingernails just like Halley. But I don't want those puffy pink pimply things on my chin."

"I'm outta here, Hubble," I said and headed for the craft box. Making jewelry sure wouldn't be my first choice but I'd do anything to keep Daisy quiet.

Button Rings

YOU'LL NEED:
- ☆ Colored pipe cleaners
- ☆ Large buttons

Tip:
You can buy bags of buttons inexpensively at a variety of stores.

We pushed pipe cleaners through the holes in the buttons to make rings.

When we had more rings than Saturn, Daisy decided we should make a necklace and bracelets to match her ring.

"Give me a break, Daisy," I told her. "Maybe you can get Halley to show you how to make a necklace like the one she's wearing."

"Sure," said Halley, "I can roll a really wicked paper necklace. Let me show you."

Nifty Necklace

YOU'LL NEED:
- ☆ Scissors
- ☆ Paper – use paper from the recycle box or fancy paper
- ☆ Straw
- ☆ Glue
- ☆ Waxed dental floss

Cut a large triangular strip of paper as shown here.

Roll tightly onto a straw.

When you near the end, run a little line of glue along the center.

Finish rolling and hold the bead long enough to make sure the glue holds.

When you have made about a dozen beads string them on to your dental floss.

Tip:
Colored dental floss is fun but string, a long shoelace, or yarn work well too.

keep tip centered

glue

Halley rolled a triangle of paper on a straw,

glued it, and strung it on dental floss.

"Now," said Daisy, "I'm going to make my very own creation. I'll make you a button bracelet, and then I'm going to string colored paper clips together and make a rainbow bracelet, and then I'm going to…."

Easy-peasy Bracelet

YOU'LL NEED:
☆ Buttons
☆ Waxed colored dental floss
☆ Scissors

Lay buttons out in a line to make a pretty pattern and arrive at the length you want.

Cut a piece of floss long enough to wrap around the wrist 2 to 3 times.

String buttons by going through both holes so it lies flat.

Tie off with a bow.

Daisy lay buttons out flat and strung the floss through the holes.

Tip:
You can also make a bracelet using a piece of ribbon and a single large pretty button and tie it on your wrist with a bow.

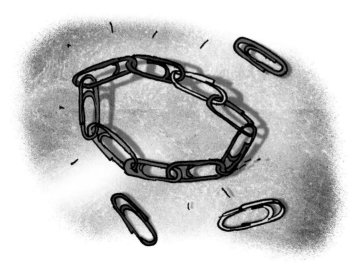

Then she strung paper clips together in a colorful Daisy chain.

This was getting to be way too much for me. I needed a challenge. I took some of the floss that they weren't using and tried to write my name.

I mastered that in a nanosecond and was ready for another challenge. So I tried to beat my switching shoelace record. On a good day I can switch my shoelaces and retie them in under two minutes.

"Maybe if you decorated them with comets and bolts of lightning you might go faster," said Halley.

Loony Laces

YOU'LL NEED:
★ Markers (permanent ones if you walk through puddles!)
★ Wide shoelaces

I spread my laces out on newspaper and used markers to decorate them.

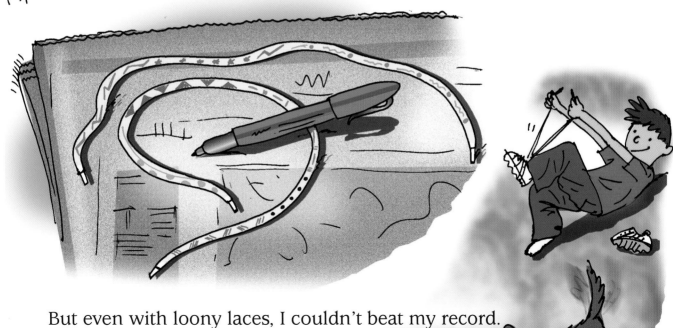

But even with loony laces, I couldn't beat my record.

Fancy Hands

"I want fancy fingernails just like you," Daisy told Halley.

"I'm not sure your mother would want me to paint your nails," said Halley.

Daisy's lip started to quiver. As fast as I could, I got out the paper and crayons.

Really Neat Nails

YOU'LL NEED:
- ☆ Paper
- ☆ Crayons
- ☆ Scissors

We outlined our hands on the paper. Halley and Daisy decorated them with rings and the fanciest nails I've ever seen.

Tip:
Use scissors to curl the ends of nails.

"Fancy fingers aren't really my thing," I said. "I'm turning mine into alien hands with curling nails and crusty scales."

"Oh no, Lee-o, don't scare Halley," cried Daisy. "I'm going to make her a beautiful hand. I'll put a ribbon through it to make a bookmark so she can take it home and show all her friends!"

Hand-y Bookmark

YOU'LL NEED:
☆ Heavy paper
☆ Crayons
☆ Scissors
☆ Long piece of ribbon

Trace your hand on the paper.
Decorate it, then cut it out.
Make a hole at the base.
String a long ribbon through the hole and tie.

Everything was A-Okay so far. But I could see that my real challenge would be keeping Daisy happy, 'cuz when Daisy's not happy—nobody is!

Space Snacks

Millennium Munch Bars

YOU'LL NEED:
- ☆ 1/2 cup (125 mL) margarine
- ☆ 1/2 cup (125 mL) flour
- ☆ 1/2 cup (125 mL) brown sugar, firmly packed
- ☆ 1–1/2 cups (375 mL) quick oats
- ☆ 1/2 tsp. (2 mL) baking soda
- ☆ 1/4 cup (50 mL) cut-up dried apricots
- ☆ 1/4 cup (50 mL) chocolate chips (op)

Put the margarine into a 9"(24 cm) square microwave-safe dish.

Microwave on High 30 seconds or until melted.

Add the rest of the ingredients to the bowl and mix thoroughly. Press evenly into dish.

Microwave on High for three minutes or until bubbly.

Cool and cut into squares.

A hungry Daisy is not a happy Daisy. Mom had left apple juice and raisins. I'll bet by the time you're old enough to be a babysitter, the same old snacks seem pretty lame. I decided to make Halley some munchies for the millennium!

"I'm going to make apricot bars just like they serve in the space station," I said.

I cut up dried apricots

and mixed them with margarine, oats, flour, and brown sugar.

Tip:
You can cut dried apricots with a pair of scissors.

Halley helped me cook them in the microwave.

"Why don't we turn the couch into a spaceship so we can eat our space bars while we orbit the earth," said Halley.

"Affirmative!!" I shouted.

"This might not be as bad as I thought," I whispered to Hubble. Except for one thing. Miss Daisy was driving me crazy! She was already loading all her toy animals onto our space capsule couch.

"Stuffed animals in space are a negative!" I shouted as I hurled Poopsie Bear overboard, just missing Mom's new lamp.

"This doesn't sound like Tranquility Base to me, Leo," said Halley.

Tranquility Base was the area of the moon where the first man landed. It was named because of its peace and quiet.

"I wonder what the astronauts, all cooped up in a capsule, do to let off steam."

"They have all kinds of special exercises," I told her, "but I'll bet they'd rather be playing basketball and so would I."

"No problem," said Halley. "We'll shoot some hoops." She got a large laundry basket and put a small wastebasket inside. We tossed rolled socks into the basket, getting extra points if we got one in the bull's-eye wastebasket.

We sunk socks until Halley decided we needed some downtime.

"How would you like to make some eerie extraterrestrials?"

Agile Aliens

YOU'LL NEED:
★ Paper
★ Markers or crayons

Draw a head at the top of a sheet of paper.

Fold the drawing back, leaving a little bit visible, and pass it to the next person.

That person continues the drawing, adding a body.

Continue folding and adding parts of the body until each person has a turn.

Open up to see what a wacky creature you've created.

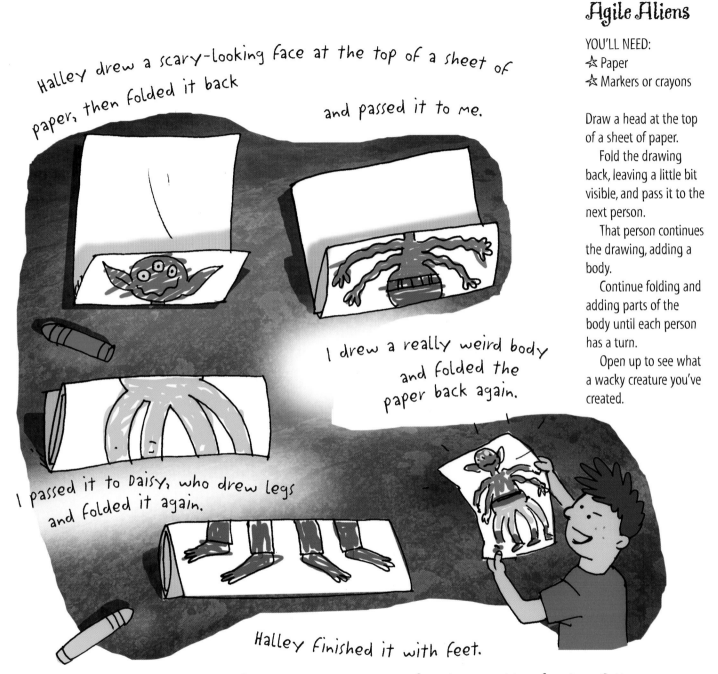

Halley drew a scary-looking face at the top of a sheet of paper, then folded it back

and passed it to me.

I drew a really weird body and folded the paper back again.

I passed it to Daisy, who drew legs and folded it again.

Halley finished it with feet.

When we unfolded the paper we found a pretty freaky fellow.

"Far out," I said. "We'll need an army of these aliens. Daisy, you go get more paper."

21

"You're not the boss of me, Leo. Besides, I've had enough of your folded friends. I want to play with my diggity dough."

"That's way too boring for Halley. I'm going to create a concoction that I know she's never seen before."

Cosmic Color Bursts

YOU'LL NEED:
- ☆ Dinner plate
- ☆ Water
- ☆ Vegetable oil
- ☆ Food coloring
- ☆ Plastic wrap

Pour a thin layer of water onto the plate.

Add a little vegetable oil, just enough to make an oil island in the middle of the water.

Squirt single drops of each color of food coloring you have at the edges of the oil island. Try a few directly on the island too.

Tear off a piece of plastic wrap larger than the plate and carefully lay it directly on the surface.

Take turns gently touching the wrap. The colors will burst and mix.

Halley pressed the colors and they magically mixed.

"Brilliant!" said Halley. "What borealic bursts of cosmic color!"

"Hubble," I said, "I think that means she's having a good time."

Launching Lunch

Getting Daisy to eat at mealtime is as tricky as turning cartwheels on the moon. If I didn't want Halley to have a major Daisy meltdown on her hands, plain old sandwiches wouldn't do. I dug out the cookie cutters and cut a gingerbread man out of a piece of bread. He looked a lot like a spaceman once I spread him with cream cheese.

I decided to use an olive for eyes and sprinkle him with sprouts.

"Why are you sprinkling him with grass?" asked Daisy.
"This isn't grass…it's Astroturf!" I told her.

Technicolor Toast

YOU'LL NEED:
- ✯ Milk
- ✯ Food coloring
- ✯ Sandwich bread
- ✯ Cotton swabs (one for each color)
- ✯ Small bowls

Measure 2 tbsp. (25mL) milk into each bowl.

Add a few drops of food coloring. Repeat with three or four colors.

Soak the cotton swab in the milk-paint and dab on the bread to create your design.

Toast.

"Oh no, Lee-o," she sputtered, "I don't want to eat that spaceman! I want a cheese and cucumber sandwich on our special painted bread."

Halley looked puzzled when I put food coloring into little bowls of milk.

We painted awesome designs on the bread and toasted it.

Halley made sandwiches with our painted toast

and turned them into beautiful butterflies.

We felt like real astronauts as we slurped our space shakes with straws stuck in plastic pouches.

Space Smoothie

FOR EACH SMOOTHIE YOU'LL NEED:
✩ 1 cup (250 mL) banana
(or any other fruit)
✩ 1/2 cup (125 mL) yogurt
✩ 1 tbsp. (15 mL) liquid honey
✩ Zip-lock bag
✩ Straw

Put fruit in a blender. Add honey and yogurt. Blend until smooth.

 Pour into a small-size zip-lock bag. Seal the bag, leaving room at the side to insert the straw.

gravity boots

Tattoo Time

While Daisy was busy finishing every last bite of her lunch, I worked on organizing my card collection.

"Forget about your dumb cards, Leo," said Daisy. "We have to think of fun things for our babysitter. I have a great idea—tattoos!"

"Yeah right, Daisy," I said."

I couldn't believe it when Halley said, "Cool. Tattoos are great! Let's make them with washable marker. I'm going to draw a flower on Daisy's cheek and I'll bet I can find the Big…and Little…Dipper in Leo's freckles."

Tip:
Try your tattoo on paper first to make sure you like it. Make extra sure your markers say washable watercolor!

"I want two tattoos too," Daisy wailed.

"It sounds like Daisy's wilting," I told Halley. "Mom would say that she's ready for some quiet time."

"Oh no, Lee-o, tattooed ladies never need quiet time," said Daisy.

"How about a little spa time then," suggested Halley. "We can all relax with a cool cosmic cucumber mask."

We washed our faces with a cold washcloth and then covered them with cool, thin slices of cucumber.

While we stretched out with the cool, slippery slices on our faces, Hubble gobbled up all the cucumber.

"Ewwww!" said Daisy, holding her nose. "Someone did something rude!"

"It's only Hubble," I said. "Cucumbers always set off his retro rockets, if you know what I mean."

I think Halley smiled but I couldn't really tell 'cuz I had cucumbers on my eyes.

"Why don't we make some frozen bananas," said Halley. "The bananas need to chill out for a while, so we will too!"

We rolled the bananas in wheat germ and poked chocolate chips all over them.

Crunchy Monkeys

YOU'LL NEED:
- ✯ 3 bananas
- ✯ 1/2 cup (125 mL) wheat germ
- ✯ Chocolate chips
- ✯ Popsicle sticks
- ✯ Plastic wrap

Peel bananas.
   Cut each in half crosswise.
   Put a popsicle stick in the flat cut end of each banana half.
   Roll each banana in wheat germ.
   Stud with chocolate chips.
   Wrap with plastic wrap and freeze.

Tip:
Make octopus eyes with two cloves or a marker.

"My bears want to play quietly in my room with me," said Daisy, "but first I'd better make an octopus from the peel to babysit the bananas so no one eats them."

Rocket Ship Flip Book

YOU'LL NEED:
- ★ At least 20 plain sheets of paper or index cards around 3" x 5" (8 cm x 12 cm)
- ★ Black marker
- ★ Metal clip

Clip the papers together. Starting with the last page, draw a simple picture in the lower part of the card, for example, a rocket ready to take off.

On the next page, draw the same thing, changing it slightly, for example, make the rocket a tiny bit farther from the ground.

Keep drawing the same picture, changing it a little bit more each time.

When you're finished put your thumb under the last page and flip the pages. The picture will start to move just like a real video!

When Halley came back from planting Daisy in her room she looked tired, but I know teenagers never get tired…they stay up really late.

"How 'bout a video," Halley yawned. "Your mom said you could watch one."

"No way," I said. "I'm in charge of seeing that you have a good time. Watching a kid's video won't be my idea of fun when I'm your age. We'll make our very own video of a rocket ship."

I drew pictures of rockets and made them into a flip book.

The Paper Bag Princess

We had just finished our flip book when Daisy appeared in her soccer uniform and crown.

"I want to be a soccer-playing princess with a beautiful braid all the way down my back," said Daisy.

Halley laughed. "You can only have a braid as long as your hair. But I can try to make two small braids."

How to Braid

Really Weird Wraps

YOU'LL NEED:
- ☆ Scissors
- ☆ Square of cardboard about 3" (7 cm)
- ☆ Thread or yarn

Cut a slit to the middle of the card and wiggle the scissors to make a small hole.

Cut a thread 3 times longer than the length of your hair.

Slip a small section of your hair through the hole and press the cardboard as close to your scalp as you can.

Tie the thread tightly in a double knot close to the cardboard.

Wind the thread tightly around the hair. Hold the hair with one hand and wind with the other.

Wind to the end. Change colors if you want. Tie each color off with a double knot.

When she finished Daisy's braids, Halley helped me wrap some of my hair into a wobbly antenna.

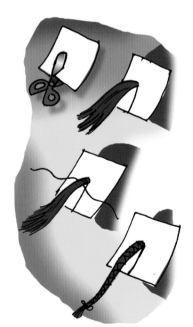

She pulled some of my hair through a cardboard square and wrapped it with colored thread.

32

"I want to learn to braid all by myself," said Daisy.
Halley told us she learned to braid on a little paper cat,
so she made one for Daisy.

We cut cats out of cardboard, made holes,
and pulled three strands of yarn through each hole.
Halley made a knot at the back and we braided the yarn into a tail.

Daisy practised and practised until she got it right. Now she wanted to braid everything. Halley showed her how to make a doll from yarn, with braided arms.

Princess Daisy Doll

YOU'LL NEED:
☆ Yarn
☆ Scissors

1. Wrap yarn around a book about 8"(20cm) wide (this book is just right) about 30 times.

2. Slip a 12" (30 cm) length of doubled yarn under the strands at the side of the book.

3. Pull tightly and tie in a double knot, then tie a bow. Slip yarn off book and cut through the bottom ends.

4. Tie a piece of yarn around doll's neck. Trim.

5. Separate out 3 strands on each side of doll for arms and braid to desired length. (If you want fatter arms separate out 12 strands on each side of doll for arms. Make 3 groups of 4 strands each and braid.)

6. Tie a piece of yarn (a rubber band or twist tie works too) around doll's wrists and waist. Trim ends.

With Daisy one thing always leads to another. "My princess doesn't have a bed!"

I figured out how to make a doll's bed and actually it was pretty neat, if I say so myself.

Paper Bag Bed

YOU'LL NEED:
- ✰ Brown paper lunch bag
- ✰ Scissors

Cut the bag in half.
Open out remaining bag. Fold the top over toward the outside twice to create bed.

Halley and Daisy decorated it with markers and stickers and soon she had a princess in a paper bag bed.

As we chomped our crunchy bananas, I looked outside.

"It's raining cats and dogs," I shouted. "I just saw a man step in a poodle." Sometimes I crack myself up with my jokes. Hubble likes them too, but I don't think Halley thinks I'm all that funny. Maybe when you get older you lose your sense of humor.

Even when I tried my very best one: "If athletes get athlete's foot, what do astronauts get?" "Missile-toe!!" She didn't laugh but she did say, "You should make a book for all your jokes."

"I can never do anything without 'Ditto Daisy' doing it too," I said.

"I think you're lucky to have your own little satellite," said Halley.

"It's more like my own little space invader!"

"Then how about if Daisy and I make our own book, so you can concentrate on yours."

Book of Secrets

YOU'LL NEED:
☆ An inexpensive notebook (not spiral bound)
☆ Scissors
☆ Stickers

1. Lay the notebook on a flat surface and lift up the lower edge of the first page and fold it along the seam where the notebook is stapled or stitched together.

2. Do the same with the upper edge of the page. The two folds bring the page to a point. Repeat, folding each page of the notebook.

3. When you have finished folding, cut down the cover with a pair of scissors. This will turn a rectangular notebook into a triangular one.

4. On each page write a secret or special quote.

5. Seal it with a sticker.

Halley and Daisy turned a plain old notebook into a really cool book.

Halley wrote secrets and poems.
Daisy decorated each page and sealed them with stickers.

I started right in creating "Leo's Out of This World Book of Jokes." No stickers for me, just a little folding and fiddling was all I'd need.

Leo's Joke Book

YOU'LL NEED:
- ☆ Paper
- ☆ Scissors
- ☆ Markers

Always fold along the dotted line in the direction of the arrows.
1. Fold paper in half.
2. Fold in half again.
3. Fold in half again!
4. Unfold twice. (It will look like Step #2.) Cut as shown.
5. Open paper all the way. Fold in half.
6. Push from the ends. Press down on folds to smooth out edges.
7. Fold into a four-page book.

Oopsie-daisy, Daisy

Mashed Potato Mountain

YOU'LL NEED:
⭐ Mound of leftover mashed potatoes (or modelling dough)
⭐ 2 tbsp.(25 mL) baking soda
⭐ 1/2 cup (125 mL) vinegar
⭐ Food coloring (op)

Push a small glass or paper cup into the center of the mound of potatoes.

Press them around the container.

Put baking soda in the cup and add a few drops of red and/or yellow food coloring on top of the baking soda.

When you're ready for the volcano, quickly pour in half of the vinegar. The lava will flow down the mountain.

When the flow stops, add more vinegar.

Halley had been stuck with Daisy for a long time making their silly book of secrets. It was time for something spectacular. I found some leftover mashed potatoes and molded them into a mountain. I knew Mom wouldn't mind since this whole babysitter thing was her idea.

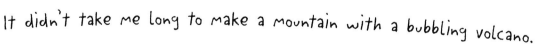
It didn't take me long to make a mountain with a bubbling volcano.

Halley was speechless as my volcano bubbled and oozed. Soon something was rumbling and it wasn't just the volcano. My stomach was telling me it was time for supper!

"Our new babysitter told me she's a vegetable," announced Daisy. "I want to be a vegetable too…a big green zucchini."

"I'm a vegetarian," corrected Halley.

I don't know a whole lot about what vegetarians eat but I know she's not going to be a big fan of biting into one of the big juicy hotdogs mom left for supper.

Solar System Salad

Smallest planet to largest:
Pluto – peppercorn
Mercury – green pea
Mars – cherry tomato
Venus – large radish
Earth – hard-boiled egg
Neptune – field tomato
Uranus – orange
Saturn – cabbage
Jupiter – lettuce

Use your imagination and whatever you have on hand for your own salad.

"We'll make a Solar System salad!!" I said. "I found a great site on the computer that shows each planet and its size compared to the others. We could sorta do the same with salad ingredients. The smallest planet, Pluto, would have to be a little peppercorn and the biggest, Jupiter, a humongous head of lettuce!"

"I'll get the egg," squealed Daisy. As she dashed for the fridge, I knew she wanted to be the one to show Halley how I crack a hard-boiled egg on my forehead before I peel it. She whipped an egg from the shelf and cracked it on her head. It only took a second before raw egg started to slither down her forehead like lava from a volcano. Daisy erupted.

Leo's Eggs-periment

YOU'LL NEED:
☆ One hard-boiled egg
☆ One raw egg

Spin each egg on its side. The hard-boiled egg will spin smoothly because it is solid.

The raw egg will hardly spin because it is slowed down by its sloshy contents.

"Oh no, Daisy-o," I said, trying not to laugh.

Halley and Hubble started in cleaning a dripping Daisy, while I took her mind off her troubles and showed her the way I tell the difference between a hard-boiled and a raw egg.

Halley and I put all the salad dressing ingredients in a plastic jar.

Then I put on Daisy's favorite CD and let her jump around and mix the ingredients while we finished the salad. In a shake she had forgotten about her eggy experience!

Daisy's Disco Dressing

YOU'LL NEED:
- ☆ 1/2 cup (125 mL) low-fat plain yogurt
- ☆ 1/2 cup (125 mL) low-fat mayonnaise
- ☆ 1 tbsp. (15 mL) milk
- ☆ 1 tsp. (5 mL) Dijon mustard
- ☆ 1/2 tsp. (2 mL) dried basil
- ☆ 1/2 tsp. (2 mL) dried oregano
- ☆ 1/2 tsp. (2 mL) dried thyme
- ☆ 1/2 tsp. (2 mL) garlic salt

Place all ingredients in a plastic jar.
 Twist on lid.
 Shake!

I decided to serve our salad in my special hat-trick bowl. I make a tortilla into a bowl, which, if you use your imagination, looks a lot like a hat. I'll make this bowl when I'm living in space and don't want to wash a lot of dishes.

The trick is in the tortilla, which I mold into a bowl and nuke in the microwave.

Hat Trick Bowl

FOR EACH BOWL YOU'LL NEED:
☆ 1 large flour tortilla

Place the tortilla between two sheets of paper towel and microwave on High for 30 seconds. Tortillas mold more easily to the bowl if they are warm.

Line the bottom of a round cereal bowl with a paper towel, then fit in the warm tortilla. It takes a little pleating and folding.

Poke the tortilla several times with a fork.

Microwave on High for one minute.

Remove the tortilla from the bowl. It will become crisper and hold its shape as it cools.

Repeat for the other bowls.

"Do you like hockey?" I asked Halley.

"Sure," she said, "doesn't everyone?"

I was going to say, "Doesn't everyone like hot-dogs"…but I didn't. Instead I said, "How would you like to help me make my famous Maple Leaf Melt?"

Maple Leaf Melt

FOR EACH MELT YOU'LL NEED:
- ✯ 1 egg
- ✯ 1 English muffin – split and toasted
- ✯ 1 slice of cheese
- ✯ Margarine
- ✯ 1 tsp. (5 mL) water
- ✯ A pinch of salt and pepper

Rub the inside of a mug with margarine.

Add 1 egg, 1 tsp. (5 mL) water, a little salt and pepper.

Stir with a fork until well mixed. Microwave on High for 30 seconds. Stir well again.

Microwave on High again until firm, about 30 seconds.

Pop out of the mug onto a toasted half of muffin.

Add the cheese and press on remaining muffin half.

Tip:
A slice of tomato or lettuce is a good addition.

I got out my special "Stanley Cup" (it's really just a coffee mug).

When the egg was ready, I popped it like a sunny yellow hockey puck onto a toasted English muffin. Then I slapshot a slab of cheese on it, put the other half of the English muffin on top, and we were ready to eat!

Halley's Comet

Yogurt-y Fruit Cones

YOU'LL NEED:
- ⭐ Ice cream cones
- ⭐ Cut-up fruit
- ⭐ 1/2 cup (125 mL) yogurt
- ⭐ 1 tbsp. (15 mL) orange juice
- ⭐ 1 tbsp. (15 mL) liquid honey

Mix yogurt, orange juice, and liquid honey together.
   Drizzle over fruit in cone.

When we finished our supper, Halley started to spoon the cut-up fruit Mom left into bowls, but I thought it would be a lot more fun served in ice cream cones.

44

By the time we'd finished, the kitchen looked like it had been caught in a cosmic hurricane.

"I'm going to make it very easy to clean up," said Halley. She wrote the clean-up and bedtime chores on sticky notes and stuck them all over us until we looked like molting Martians.

Each time we finished a job we could take off a note. One of mine was "wash dishes" but thanks to our edible bowl and ice cream cone dishes there wasn't much to do.

Hubble's Bubbles

YOU'LL NEED:
- ✯ 4 tbsp. (60 mL) of dishwashing liquid
- ✯ 1/2 cup (125 mL) warm water
- ✯ 1 tsp. (5 mL) sugar
- ✯ Straws
- ✯ Rubber band

Mix dishwashing liquid and sugar with water.

Wrap a rubber band around three or four straws.

Dip into the mixture and blow gently.

My sink full of dishes gave Daisy the idea of bubbles before bedtime.

"Blowing bubbles isn't exactly rocket science," I complained to Hubble, "but he was too happy breaking bubbles to hear."

Halley poured some of the dishwashing liquid onto a plate and added water.

Then she wrapped a rubber band around some straws and we blew billions of bubbles.

Hubble was snoring as if he didn't have a problem in the world. I lay in bed staring up at the solar system on my ceiling and thinking that having a new babysitter wasn't so bad at all. I was even hoping that, unlike Halley's comet, this Halley would come back more often than every 76 years.

Just then, Halley peeked in and said it was time to turn out the lights.

"I sure hope you had a good time today," I said.

"I had a blast. I hope your mom calls me again soon."

"I'll bet you didn't know that Halley is a comet's name," I said as she headed for the door.

Halley just smiled her shiny smile and turned out the light.

We acknowledge the support of the Canada Council for the Arts, the Ontario Arts Council, the Government of Ontario through the Ontario Book Publishers Tax Credit program and the Ontario Book Initiative, and the Government of Canada through the Book Publishing Industry Development Program (BPIDP) for our publishing activities.

Cataloging in Publication Data

Hunter, Dette, 1943-
    38 ways to entertain your babysitter / by Dette Hunter ; art by Stephen MacEachern.

ISBN 1-55037-795-7 (bound).—ISBN 1-55037-794-9 (pbk.)

1. Indoor games—Juvenile literature. 2. Handicraft—Juvenile literature.
3. Cookery—Juvenile literature. 4. Babysitters—Juvenile literature.
I. MacEachern, Stephen II. Title.

TT160.H857 2003   j793   C2003-900515-1

The art in this book was hand drawn, scanned, and colored in Photoshop®.

Distributed in Canada by:
Firefly Books Ltd.
3680 Victoria Park Avenue
Willowdale, ON
M2H 3K1

Published in the U.S.A. by Annick Press (U.S.) Ltd.
Distributed in the U.S.A. by:
Firefly Books (U.S.) Inc.
P.O. Box 1338
Ellicott Station
Buffalo, NY 14205

Printed and bound in Belgium.

Visit us at: www.annickpress.com

Neither the publisher nor the author shall be liable for any damage that may be caused or sustained as a result of conducting any of the activities in this book without specifically following instructions, conducting the activities without proper supervision, or ignoring the cautions in this book.

Acknowledgments
I thank my three children, Chris, Sarah and Mary, and all the other babies and babysitters in my life for their input and inspiration, and of course, Sheryl Shapiro and Annick Press.
                                                                —*Dette Hunter*